All I Want
for Christmas
Is You

All I Want for Christmas Is You

A collection of love poems
From Blue Mountain Arts®

Blue Mountain Press ®

Boulder, Colorado

Library of Congress Catalog Card Number: 93-21906
ISBN: 0-88396-372-8

ACKNOWLEDGMENTS appear on page 62.

⊓ design on book cover is registered in
U.S. Patent and Trademark Office.

Manufactured in the United States of America
First Printing: August, 1993

Library of Congress Cataloging-in-Publication Data

All I want for Christmas is you: a collection of love poems from Blue
    Mountain Arts.
        p.   cm.
    ISBN 0-88396-372-8 : $15.95
    1. Love poetry, American. 2. Christmas—Poetry. I. Blue
Mountain Arts (Firm)
PS595.L6A44   1993   93-21906
811'.54080354—dc20   CIP

Blue Mountain Press ®

P.O. Box 4549, Boulder, Colorado 80306

CONTENTS

Merry Christmas,
My Love

I wanted to get you
   something special for Christmas.

I didn't want something that
   would wear out or get used up.
I wanted something that
   would last,
something you could
   take with you wherever you go.

At last, I thought of something
that is all of the things I wanted:
it won't ever wear out,
you can't use it up,
it will last forever,
and you can take it with you
   everywhere.
It's something no one else
   can give you:

   my heart, my love.

—Deloras Ann Lane

I can't begin to tell you how
wonderful it is . . . to be sharing
this season . . . with you.

Presents aren't the only things
that get opened up around
Christmastime.
So do people's emotions. And their
most sincere and special feelings.

And one of the feelings
I want to offer, so warmly, to you
is just how very much I love you.

Let me say that I never
want you to wonder —
   this Christmas or any other —
     about my feelings for you.

I want you to feel safe and secure
in the knowledge that
   my love is all for you,
     and it always will be.

When you already have the best . . .
   the rest just don't seem
     to matter.

And I do have the best . . . in you.

—Carey Martin

The priceless gifts of Christmas
are not the ones wrapped
or placed under the tree,
but the gifts we give when
we give of ourselves.
It is the love that we share.
It is the comfort we lend at times of need.
It is the moments we spend together
helping each other follow our dreams.

The most priceless gifts of Christmas
are the understanding and caring
that come from the heart.
And each and every one of us
has these gifts to offer . . .
through the gift of ourselves.

—Ben Daniels

I Want to Say More than Just "I Love You"

Sometimes it's not enough just
    to say "I love you."
Even though I do love you,
I feel I need to express more,
because there is so much more
    to our relationship.
Sometimes I need to tell you that
you're the love I live for,
you're my dream made into reality.
Yours are the arms that
hold me close,
and it is your smile that brings
a ray of sunshine
to even the darkest of days.

You are the one who tells me
to keep believing in myself,
in you, and in us.
You have become a part of me
I could never live without,
and as long as I'm living,
as long as you care,
I'll be here for you.
I'll do anything for you.
This is a special time in our lives,
because we are sharing it together.
I love you.

—Janine Stahl

I thank you. So much.
My thoughts thank you.
My smile thanks you.
And my brighter days thank you.

Thank you.
For making more than a difference.
For taking more than just the time.
Thank you for doing . . . all that you
        so wonderfully do.

I wish I could express the gratitude
I feel in so many different ways.
It's hard to say the meaningful things;
the words that come to mind
usually find themselves falling short
of the feelings that I'd like to share
and the things I'd like to say.

But I want you to know that
"thanks" is one emotion
that flows directly into the heart.

And it's a very wonderful feeling
        that never goes away.

—Casey Whilson

This is such a special time of year.
Sparkling lights on beautiful pine trees,
holiday food and brightly wrapped gifts.
But you are the most wonderful gift
   for me.
Your smiles and laughter always
bring me good cheer.
Your gentle touch and warm embrace
always light up my heart.
Your sweet understanding
   and concern
always fill me with joy.

Being with you at Christmas makes me
more cheerful and joyful.
And I am hoping that this merry season
brings you peace and happiness.
I wish that your every dream
will be fulfilled,
and that every day in the new year
will be full of health and good feelings.
Most of all, I wish you love,
and I want you to know that
I love and appreciate you
more than I can say.

—Donna Levine

If I were to make you a Christmas stocking,
I'd fill it with these gifts
from within my heart:
First, I would give my love
without expectation or condition,
and add a little tenderness
to last throughout the year.
Next, I'd add forgiveness
for mistakes that may be made
and sprinkle it with understanding
to help when you're unsure.
I'd give to you my friendship
for times when you feel alone,
along with my laughter and a smile
for when you cannot find your own.
In a very special part,
I would place my faith and trust
to guide you through times of doubt.
And finally, I'd place my heart
in the center of it all
to love you for all the years to come.

—Amy Michele Shockey

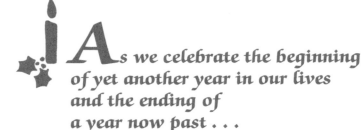

As we celebrate the beginning
of yet another year in our lives
and the ending of
a year now past . . .

Somehow, nothing I could
    say or do
seems quite enough.
This season doesn't just
symbolize the passing of one more year.
It symbolizes another year of our lives
that we chose to spend together.

In the year we're now putting behind us,
you gave so much of yourself.
Your patience, your understanding,
    and your love
helped me through each rough moment
    we experienced,
and the memories and dreams
    we shared together
added new meaning to my life.

In the year that has passed,
    we grew closer.
Our relationship grew stronger,
and we learned that it takes tears
    as well as laughter
to build a love that is worthwhile
and that will endure no matter what
    the future holds.
We learned that, together,
    we can face anything.

That's why nothing
    seems adequate enough
to sum up the meaning and the true
importance of the year
that has now come to an end.
There are no words that can
come close to describing my thoughts,
    my feelings, or my gratitude
for you and our relationship.
So I'll simply say, "Thank you,"
for the precious year
we have just spent together
and the many more years
and holiday seasons
that we have yet to share.

—Deanne Laura Gilbert

One of the best
presents that a person
can give or receive
is memories.
Memories are never returned,
never take up room
or need to be replaced,
and they always fit just right.

—Vicki Perkins

Within my heart,
in a certain place where
my favorite memories
and my happiest hopes
and my nicest thoughts are,
there is a space that belongs
just to you.

—Barin Taylor

At Christmas and Always, Remember This . . .

I don't expect perfection from you,
   for I respect who you are,
and I don't expect you not to fail sometimes,
   for you are just as human as I am.
I don't seek to know all your secrets,
   for I know that you are an individual,
and I don't ask that you fill all my needs,
   for I understand that you have hopes
   and dreams of your own.

I don't question your strength,
    for I know how far you've come,
and I don't expect you to
    carry every burden alone,
    for I am here
    to go through it all with you.
I don't ask that you possess all the answers,
    for I know there will be times
    when you're as unsure as I am.
I only ask that you let me be your friend
    when you need strength or laughter,
    your partner when it comes to our dreams
        and our future,
    and your comfort when you need to forget
        the world outside.
And always I ask that you remember
    how much I love you.

—Jennifer Nelson-Fenwick

Year after year,
we see ourselves change,
and the world changes around us.
We are never the same
from day to day,
and we experience life
in so many ways.
At times, it challenges us
with unexpected difficulties,
but we become stronger
and more self-sufficient;
we learn how to depend on ourselves
and rely on one another.

You and I
have come to understand
that even if life
is not always perfect,
when we have each other
to enjoy the better moments,
it doesn't have to be perfect
to be special.

—Laura Medley

We Don't Need to Wish that We Were Rich This Christmas...

Because We Already Are!

How many times have we
sat around and talked about
all the things
we would do if somehow
we were to win the lottery?
How many times have we dreamed
of the thousands of ways
we could spend a million dollars?
How many times
have we said to each other,
"If only we were rich . . ."?

Well, this Christmas,
I won't go so far as to say
that it wouldn't be nice
to win that lottery
or to have a million dollars.
But, you know,
there really are some things
that money just can't buy —
like love and laughter,
sunshine and smiles,
a feeling of security,
and someone like you to love.

—Taylor MacKenzie

If I could hold all my feelings for you
in my hand,
I would wrap them in brightly colored
Christmas paper
and tie them with beautiful ribbons
and bows.
Then I would place them under the
Christmas tree for you to open.
And you would unwrap them,
holding them up to the light
so you could see their many facets
and watch them sparkle.
Then you would know
just how strong and deep
my love is for you.

—Judith L. Sloan

Let's Try to Spend
Some Quiet Time Together
This Holiday Season

Every year at this time we seem
to get so frantic preparing for the
Christmas season that we end up
too busy to enjoy all the true
pleasures it holds.
Shopping, baking, decorating,
more shopping . . .
too many of these activities
crowd out some of the warmth
and joy that Christmas is all about.

That's why this year I want to take
some time amidst the chaos — right in
the middle of creating a memorable
Christmas for those we love — to
enjoy each other.
I want to stop and breathe in the scent
of freshly cut pine boughs. I want to
sit up late listening to our favorite
carols. I want to reminisce about our
first Christmas together . . . and every
one since.
When I look into your eyes, I see all the
excitement and anticipation that
make this our favorite time of year.
So let's take time to experience that
joy. Let's start a new holiday tradition
by spending a few stolen moments of
quiet time together. We will be giving
each other something truly priceless —
memories that last a lifetime.

—Pamela Koehlinger

My Christmas Dream

It's a moonlit night, the air is crisp,
and a wondrous white landscape is
all around us. There we are, walking
hand in hand, lifting our faces
to the falling bits of snow.
Colored lights flicker around
us; their warm tones reflect
from snow-covered pine boughs,
and the beauty of this moment
becomes a silent wonder.
I feel your hand in mine,
and in that moment, I have
everything that I could wish for.
Though our faces are red with cold,
our spirits feel renewed and our
love feels more alive and fresh
than ever before.
It's a moonlit night, the air is crisp,
and a wondrous white landscape is
all around us. There we are,
walking hand in hand together . . .
more in love than ever.

—Linda Sackett-Morrison

What Is It About Christmas That Makes Me Love You Even More?

I seem to fall in love with you all over again at Christmastime.

Maybe it's the excitement
of surprising you with a gift.
Maybe it's because I feel
   closer to you
when we come together on holidays
and share our family traditions.
Maybe it's the romance
   of the season,
the candlelight and fireplaces.

Or maybe, just maybe,
it's simply you.

—Amy Michele Shockey

Christmas is the bringing together of
our most heartfelt and happy thoughts.
It is thinking of those we care so
much about. It is the cherishing of
memories through the years, and it is
looking forward to the blessings that lie ahead.

Christmas is the quiet appreciation
of times together, of making
everything better, and of feelings that glow
like candles in the window. Christmas is
a time of the year that has been so golden in
its yesterdays and is so hopeful as it
travels on its way towards tomorrow.

Christmas is a prayer that keeps us
close and blesses us with a gentle
recognition of all that we are.

Christmas is you and me in this world,
    wishing on the very same star.

—D. Pagels

Every Day with You
Is like Christmas

Especially at Christmastime,
I think about your smile
and I think about your laughter.
I think about the sweet things
you say and do,
and I think about my happiness
when I am with you.

I remember our special moments together,
and I remember the times that were hard.
I remember your faith in me
and my trust in you,
and I remember your gentleness,
your encouragement, and your love.
And I realize that every day with you
is like Christmas.

—Donna Levine

I Wish We
Could Spend Every Single Minute
of Christmas Together

I wish you were here to share
every moment with me;
to lean against the windowsill
and laughingly press your nose against
the frosty pane;
to look at me with eyes so bright
and so inviting,
challenging me
to step outside with you
into another world —
a world of tranquility and peace,
  a world for lovers.

I wish you were here
to share the beauty,
to take away the chill
that the fire cannot touch,
to offer me the warmth of your touch
and your kiss.

I wish you were here every minute,
so we could count each snowflake
and marvel at its beauty.
I wish we could act like children
racing in the snow,
building snowmen,
laughing at snowballs that hit the mark
and at the snow that clings
to our smiles and our faces.

I wish you were here,
because without you
the fire is not so bright,
not quite as warm.
The snow is not nearly as beautiful,
and although I want to so much,
I can't seem to enjoy the Christmas-card scenery
as much as I'd like to.
Staring out my window,
I wish you were here to share
every moment of Christmas . . .
to love and to make me smile.

—Deanne Laura Gilbert

I Want to Spend
Every Christmas
in Your Arms

The best place I have ever known
is in your arms.
It's a place that can clear my mind
of all thoughts,
except those wonderful ones
of you and me together at last.
It's a place that is warm,
secure, and comfortable.
It's a place where
I can be without worry.
It's a place I know I can always
go to when I need a friend
or just someone to talk to.

More than anywhere else in the world,
in your arms
is where I want to spend
every Christmas.

—Scott R. Rarick

My World Is Brightened
by Christmas Lights
and Your Love

Christmas is one of the
most beautiful times of the year.
Throughout the cities and towns,
multicolored lights adorn streets,
houses, and Christmas trees everywhere.
There is something very magical
and wonderful about those lights.
All of us feel a certain personal way
about what those lights really mean
in our lives.

I absolutely love to sit in a darkened room,
with nothing but the Christmas lights
blinking on the tree,
and quietly think about my life.

As I sit and reminisce,
I really feel thankful for you
and for the part of my life that
you touch with your love.
You have always meant so much to me,
and you always will, because
you are so understanding and honest.
I feel so comfortable when we are together,
and we have shared so many great times.

So, as Christmas comes to our lives again,
I want you to know that I am thinking
about you and about all the things
that you want to come true.
With all of my heart, I wish them for you.

—Deanna Beisser

As long as I have you this Christmas,
I will want nothing more.
My mind will be thoughtful,
and whatever I see will be beautiful.
My heart will be happy
   with the knowledge
   that you are close
   and at peace,
      with any worries far away.

My happiness, my dreams,
   my needs
   will be fulfilled in all
   you give me,
and my gratitude will be
   pure and immense.
As long as I have you this Christmas,
   I have the most precious,
      most elegant,
         most lasting
            gift on earth.

—Carol A. Oberg

The love we share
is more than ordinary love.
We do things for each other
that make our love
so much fun.
Giving to you,
and making you happy,
makes me feel happy, too.
You are truly wonderful.
You have a gentle heart
that I promise never to hurt.

I treasure our openness
and our heart-to-heart talks;
they are so special to me.
I have shared with you
all that I truly am;
I have given you my truest feelings.
Above all, I cherish us —
knowing that you are a part of me
and I am a part of you.
I am very fortunate
to have you in my life.
You are the one person
I will never forget,
the companion I will
always share things with,
and the one I will love forever.

—Kristina L. Dobbins

You are my very own Christmas miracle.
I love you so much.
You're such a tremendous part
   of my hopes and dreams,
and it seems like they keep
coming more and more true
   the longer I know you.

I love everything about you. I love
your eyes and the way I get lost in
them. I love your thoughts and the
ways you express them. I love the way
your hands are made to fit together
with mine. I love the way your spirit
brightens my world and makes every
single thing better.

I love the way we always do
the best we can to make our little
corner of the world a place where
closeness counts for everything
and where smiles shine throughout.

You're my very own miracle.
   You're what love is all about.

—Laurel Atherton

My Christmas Promise . . .

I Will Always Be
in Love with You

When you take me gently
   in your arms,
when you smile at me,
and when you reach for my hand . . .
I fall in love with you
   all over again.

Because I can trust you with my
   most private thoughts,
because you show me respect,
and because you accept me
   for who I am . . .
I fall in love with you all over again.

Because of the way we dream together,
share together, grow together,
the way that we are the light
    in each other's life,
the way that we are companions
    and best friends . . .
I fall in love with you
    all over again.

In the strength of your character,
in the sound of your laughter,
in the tender way you care . . .
I fall in love with you all over again.

As we grow older together,
as we continue to change with age,
there is one thing that will never change . . .
I will always keep falling in love with you.

—Karen Clodfelder

If I could have
a wish come true . . .

I would wish for
nothing but wonderful things
   to come
      to you.

In your life, which is
   so precious to me,
may troubles, worries, and problems
never linger; may they only make you
that much stronger and able and wise.

And may you rise each day with sunlight
in your heart, success in your path,
answers to your prayers,
   and that smile
      — that I love to see —
         always there . . . in your eyes.

—Carey Martin

My Christmas wish for you
is that there will always be
someone special by your side —
someone to share everyday things with,
who will make every holiday
   a little cheerier,
every birthday a little happier,
and every sunny day a little brighter
   just by being there.

My Christmas wish for you
is that you will always have
someone to touch your heart
and fill you with tenderness,
   love, and passion,
someone who knows when to
   stand close
and when to stand back,
yet is always just a touch away.

My Christmas wish for you
is a special someone
to fill all the days of your life
with hope, inspiration, comfort,
    and never-ending love.

And my Christmas wish for me
is to always be
that special someone
    in your life.

—Bettie Meeks

My New Year's Resolution
Is to Love You Even More

In the new year,
I want to tell you "I love you"
   more often.
I plan on loving you not only
   throughout the year ahead,
but for many years to come.
I want to spend my life caring for you
   and having you care for me, too.
I want you to know that you are
   the most important person in my life,
and that your happiness is what
   makes me happy.

This new year is going to be
   one of the best years ever,
not because I'm going to promise
   to lose weight
or write to everyone more often
   and then not do it,
but because I am going to say
   "I love you"
   with all my heart.

You'll see that this resolution
is one that I'll gladly keep.

—Dena DiIaconi

All I Want for Christmas Is You

These days, it seems that many people
have forgotten the true meaning
of Christmas.
So much importance is placed
on the giving of gifts.
I don't want it to be like that
  for us.
Don't worry about finding
  just the right gift for me;
what I want for us can't
  be found in any store,
it can't be bought or sold.
What's truly important
  are our moments shared,
the little things we do
  for each other just because we care.

No gift this Christmas
could equal the memories
we'll make together
    during this holiday season.
These memories will be with us forever,
lifetime gifts that no one
    can take away.
So please don't worry
    about what to give me for Christmas,
because nothing could
    be more precious or treasured
than what we already have:
    our hopes, our dreams, our love.

—Deanne Laura Gilbert

ACKNOWLEDGMENTS

The following is a partial list of authors whom the publisher especially wishes to thank for permission to reprint their works.

Pamela Koehlinger for "Let's Try to Spend Some Quiet Time. . . ." Copyright © 1993 by Pamela Koehlinger. All rights reserved. Reprinted by permission.

Linda Sackett-Morrison for "My Christmas Dream." Copyright © 1993 by Linda Sackett-Morrison. All rights reserved. Reprinted by permission.

Amy Michele Shockey for "What Is It About Christmas. . . ." Copyright © 1993 by Amy Michele Shockey. All rights reserved. Reprinted by permission.

Donna Levine for "Every Day with You. . . ." Copyright © 1993 by Donna Levine. All rights reserved. Reprinted by permission.

Deanne Laura Gilbert for "I Wish We Could Spend. . . ." Copyright © 1993 by Deanne Laura Gilbert. All rights reserved. Reprinted by permission.

Deanna Beisser for "My World Is Brightened. . . ." Copyright © 1993 by Deanna Beisser. All rights reserved. Reprinted by permission.

Karen Clodfelder for "My Christmas Promise. . . ." Copyright © 1993 by Karen Clodfelder. All rights reserved. Reprinted by permission.

Dena Dilaconi for "My New Year's Resolution. . . ." Copyright © 1993 by Dena Dilaconi. All rights reserved. Reprinted by permission.

A careful effort has been made to trace the ownership of poems used in this anthology in order to obtain permission to reprint copyrighted materials and to give proper credit to the copyright owners. If any error or omission has occurred, it is completely inadvertent, and we would like to make corrections in future editions provided that written notification is made to the publisher:

BLUE MOUNTAIN PRESS, INC., P.O. Box 4549, Boulder, Colorado 80306.